WAKE UP THE MACHINES!

WAKE UP THE MACHINES!

Short Stories by Caedmon College Whitby Creative Writing Club Enrichment Group

2015

Produced by

Electraglade Press

electraglade press

for

Caedmon College Whitby

WAKE UP THE MACHINES!

© Caedmon College Whitby and Electraglade Press 2015

No part of this book may be reproduced, stored in a retrieval system or transmitted in any form, by any means electronic, mechanical, audio-visual recording or otherwise without the prior permission of the individual authors and Electraglade Press.
The individual copyright of each story remains with the author of that story. The collection in its current format is copyright of
Caedmon College Whitby and Electraglade Press©2015

Cover image: Humananiality © electraglade press
From a photograph by Richard Jemison

www.electragladepress.com

Contents

Introduction   by Steve Brindle

Stories:

Love is Blind   by Beth Tiplady
Flight School   by Callum Marsay
Journey of a Life Time   by Amy Rose Gibson
Brat Camp   by Chelsea Schmalstieg
Humanania   by Heather McCarthy
The Goblin King   by Joshua Taylor
Murderer   by Kieron Marshall
Burnt Ted   by Kelsey Eddington
The Fairground   by Aurora Lindley
Attack on Titan   by Laura Gibson
We Were Soldiers   by Mark Hall
If I Wake Up   by Poppy Williams
The Machine   by Tom Noble

An Introduction by Steve Brindle

It is with great pleasure I present the short stories produced by the Year 9 Creative Writing group that I have been coaching every Wednesday afternoon for the past year. I hope the book, provides pleasure, pride and encouragement for the students as they embark upon their GCSEs proper - and in years to come, when they remember their school days (with, I hope, deep affection).

When I first met the group in September, I had two questions for them. The first was, "Why did you choose the creative writing option?" The second was, "What are you hoping to get from it?" The answers to the first question did not fill me with encouragement ("We didn't, this was our second/third/last choice") but their answers to the second question were pleasingly positive; they all seemed to want to extend their knowledge and writing skills. I believe that some of them have certainly done this to a very impressive extent, and all have gained insight into many aspects of writing, planning, editing, working to deadlines and being part of a team.

In the first term, we read and discussed many genres of short story. They then had a choice of what to write for themselves – and you can read the results in this compilation. The writers came from different English groups, with different interests, talents, experience and levels of enthusiasm. Some have produced ideas and writing of a standard that would bring them A or A* at GCSE and their ideas are worthy of publication. Some have, for the first time, structured correct dialogue and paragraphs and written developed and detailed accounts. Both kinds of writer should be commended for their excellent efforts. The collection also includes a story by a year 7 pupil who attended the CCW Creative Writing Club after school - 'Burnt Ted', inspired by the club's mascot, a burnt and battered teddy bear! A version of this story was to be included in a Grim Tales collection of 100 word stories published by Young Writers press and which includes 50 stories from Caedmon College Whitby pupils. However, the highly imaginative tale was deemed 'too violent' for that collection. We thought it of enough literary merit and value to be published and so have decided to include it here.

I wish the Caedmon College Creative Writers the very best for the future. I hope they can embark upon careers that bring them happiness and fulfilment. I do hope that from here they continue to enjoy reading and writing throughout their lives!

Mr S. Brindle. July 2015.

Love is Blind
by Beth Tiplady

My favourite colour is yellow, which is ironic actually, because I can't even see. But anyway, this story isn't even about me. It's about her, the love of my life, the apple of my eye, the sunshine that brightens even my darkest nightmare. Her skin feels like silk or the softest cashmere - and so do her lips. She's just the right height to lean on as well, about 5'4'. And her figure, wow, it's a perfect hour glass, out-in-out. She has hair that flows in perfect waves and falls all the way down to her waist. That's what her mum tells me. But to her, it's a different story. She's short, chubby and has hair the colour of mud. I can't believe a word she says. She's the most beautiful girl I will never see. She wants to be a writer and you can tell, by the way she shows me the world, with words. She describes the trees, and the birds that perch their frail bodies on the long and twisted branches, and how their feathers flow in the breeze like the leaves dotted around them. She describes people, too. People like me. She describes me with love; I can hear it in her voice. In her eyes, I have the most adorable hair that is the colour of mahogany with a little patch of white, right on the top of my head, which really brings out the white in my eyes I usually joke. She can even describe colour, which is amazing. I can still remember what some colours look like, but others I'm not so clear on. My favourite thing she describes is the sky. She could talk for days and I wouldn't stop her. I love every syllable that comes out of her mouth.

When she first started to describe things to me she wasn't very good at it. Clouds are like candy floss, floating in the sky. The way that candy floss tastes, is how clouds look. They can be small and wispy or as big as mountains. They can even change colour. The bad clouds, the ones that bring storms, are usually black but regular clouds are bright white, little balls of purity in the sky. Floating along without a care in the world. It was like she was talking to a child.

But then she started to get better at writing. The night sky is beautiful as well. Well, how she tells me it is. The day she told me about it, we were lying under a tree covered in white blossom with pale pink prints dotted around them. It was late spring, around May 27th and we laid there all day, just enjoying each other's silence. Yet when the first stars started to appear I couldn't get a word in edgeways and I wouldn't have stopped her talking if I could. She says the sky is lifeless for a while but then it springs to life. It's like the stars are all afraid to show their faces and they're all waiting for one brave star to go first. She said they were twinkling, flashing as if they each wanted to be the brightest star in the sky. I don't really remember how 'twinkle' looks so I asked her and that's when she began to string her beautiful words together again, one by one. She said it's like the sound of a clinking glass on New Year's Day, like the feeling of pins and needles running all along your leg, like popping candy dancing on your tongue and it's like the sound of an audience after an actor's best performance of the year.

Even though I love the sky, the most amazing thing she does is the colour thing. I mean she could win awards. I don't completely understand in my head what the colours look like but I feel it in my heart.

Red is her favourite colour. It's the colour of her lips when she calls my name. When she lays her hand in mine it's the feeling of my heart beating. My cheeks burn red when she says those three words. When I kiss her cheek it's the trace you want to leave etched into her heart. It's the colour of her skirt as she spins round the room, without a care in the world. Red is truly the colour of love. Yet, in my dreams, red is the colour of hate, the colour of utter despair. When she pulls her hand from mine it's the lines that her nails leave on my skin, like a sentence that will never be finished. When I find her with another, it's the colour that I breathe. When you hear her for the first time after that night it's the colour of her lies, 'It's not what it looks like'. When she smashes a glass it's the sound of the pieces forcing their way into the floor. When I scream at the top of my lungs it's the taste of blood in my mouth. It's the sound of her tears hitting the floor, piercing the silence. It's the feeling of my heart draining all the love I thought we shared as you drop to your knees. When I have nothing left, it is the colour I see when she leaves. She would never leave me, I hope. If she left me I would never be able to stop crying, if my stupid eyes would ever work. Oh, by the way, I'm blind. Since I was 4. It's a not tragic story, which is definitely not interesting. My late 'father' drunkenly crashed our car. I was flung out of my car seat. Serious head trauma. That was the last time I saw him. The last time I saw anyone in fact. The rest is history.

Yellow is the colour I feel most. I love the colour, it's the happiest colour of them all. When I hear her voice every morning she makes me glow with happiness. Yellow doesn't have a sad side, like red or green. It never gets down, sort of like me. Nothing anyone says can get me down anymore because I know that the people that have ugly personality, have an ugly exterior. And even if they don't it'll show one day in how lonely they are. People who give off bad vibes usually give of a muddy green colour. But all the people I love give off the colour yellow the lights that guide me through my dark life. She's an even brighter yellow and I wouldn't change anything about her. Apart from one thing.

I wish one day she would describe herself the way she describes the sun and the stars.

Flight School
by Callum Marsay

Norman was awoken to the sound of his alarm, which echoed through his mind like a siren in the night. He sat up with a stiff motion and gently rubbed his eyes and coughed into a rag. He stumbled over to his wardrobe and picked out a clean RAF uniform, buttoned up his khaki top and pulled on his matching trousers; Norman adjusted his RAF visor hat and pushed weakly through his tent flap. As soon as he set foot out of the make-shift doors he was immediately greeted by the sound of soldiers on their morning march. He walked briskly over to his command station and opened the familiar old rusting door. He had to thrust his whole body into it to get the old thing to open.

He sat down. His assistant, Martha, ran in and handed him a coffee-stained pile of paper. He sighed as he sorted out his papers into a pile of important and less important documents. His eyes widened as he came across a file that had 'TOP SECRET' printed on it in red ink. It had an image of a map with some foreign insurgents hunched around what looked to be a shot down RAF plane in a field. On the next page it gave the details of the missing pilots. They were Sgt Commander Wilson and Captain Arnold. He must find them and he must save them.

The next day he was awoken by his commander in charge, Sgt Brian Peppers. He immediately stood to attention, he was told he could put together a recon team to fly out to Southern France and rescue the fallen comrades. He quickly sorted out his uniform and packed an overnight bag that consisted of a toothbrush, toothpaste, a flannel, a spare RAF shirt, some clean nightclothes, a torch and a Walther P38 pistol. He admitted to himself that he was quite scared and nervous but he tried his very best not to show those emotions. Because it was before the sun rose, the small recon group could move swiftly around the RAF base without being noticed by anyone. He and Captain Arnold clambered in to the mk1 spitfire plane and turned all of the interior lights off except from the button lights. This would help them fly across the skies without being seen by the enemies on the ground. The plane was painted a gloss black colour so when they were flying at night they would be virtually invisible. The plan for them was difficult but with their expertise it could be over and done within a matter of minutes. Get in, rescue them, and get straight back out.

So at 04:00 hours only October 1942, a team of brave RAF pilots set off.

Overall there was three planes carrying a total of six people, each complete with two Thompson M1928A1 machine guns and a spare sixty magazines. Each pilot was equipped with his own Walther P38 pistol with 100 rounds of bullets, they also have seven fragment grenades. Three of the six pilots have also got standard edition pocket knives, and the other three have precision throwing knives.

Suddenly in plane No. 3 a red warning light flashed up in the cockpit, it indicated that the plane was running low on fuel. This was a major malfunction because it meant when the pilots had to land in Hungary, the would either have to risk landing or crash land, but the problem was, if they were forced to crash land then they wouldn't be able to take off again and they would have to risk the lives of yet more people because they would have to be extracted. The only alternative would be that one of the two pilots would have to crawl into the shell bay, lift up the engine cover and try and fix the broken fuel line and top it up with more, but there was another problem... The fuel was highly flammable and if a spark was created, then the whole plane would erupt into violent flames.

The planes were travelling in radio silence, and at 13:07 hours, plane 3 had to tell the other two what was wrong, the other two advised the third plane to fix the problem immediately, and that's what they did. The co-pilot of plane 3 was a doctor; Doctor Wilcox. He was a young, athletic man and he was down in the shell bay, prising off the engine cover within seconds, but when he got to the real task he was presented with a monumental problem. The fuel line had punctures in three different places. Dr. Wilcox shouted up towards the cockpit.

'Hey, Jim, it's a lot worse than what we thought down here. There's no chance of me fixing this before the fuel runs out!' James Remington replied with a simple, 'Do you think we'll make it?'

'I honestly don't know mate, we could get there and land perfectly but would we make it back to base and land safely there?'

'Argh, well have we got a spare line?'

'Honestly Jim, if we had a spare one, would I be faffing around trying to fix this one?'

'Well you know what I mean, have we got any old inner tubes or something like that hanging around this plane?'

'Wait! I've just thought! We have got an inner tube for the planes tyres but I don't know if it will be long enough to stretch from the two ends of the engine?'

'Where is it?!'

'Have a look where the wheels fold up and if no one has moved anything then it should still be there.'

'We're in luck my friend!'

'Well thank the Lord Jesus for that!'

Dr. Wilcox ripped the inner tube in half in the neatest way he could, then he got the duct tape out of the cockpit cubby hole. Now this was the part that was the trickiest, he had to take off the old fuel line and put the new one on without losing too much fuel. He took a deep breath and blocked everything out of his mind, then he unscrewed the that was holding the fuel line in place and pulled the line out as quickly as he could, he had just put the end of the inner tube on the petrol tank when he heard a shout from the front of the plane, it was Jim.

'Hey Wilky! I've just got a warning light telling me that we are running out of fuel!'

'Yeah just give me a second mate, I'll have it sorted.'

'Alright, but make it as quick as possible, we can't afford to lose fuel.' And with that said Dr. Wilcox pulled off the other end of the punctured line and replaced that with the inner tube, they were in luck, the tube fit... but only just. He re-fitted the holder in which the makeshift fuel line fit inside, and placed the engine cover back onto the hole in the floor. He went back up to the cockpit and told Jim how everything went perfectly. Jim was ecstatic, he shook Dr. Wilcox's hand and got on with the flying.

A few hours later they were directly above where the files said the plane should be, and it was. They broke radio silence and decided where to land. In the end, they landed at an old farm house and left the planes on the track leading up to it. They took refuge inside the abandoned house and thought up a plan on how to rescue the pilots without causing any casualties, but at that moment the door was kicked in and there were guns pointed at their heads.

Journey of a Life Time
by Amy Rose Gibson

The cold wind blistered my face as I walked across a bridge, the rain soaked through my coat. I peered over the side of the bridge and stared at the murky bottomless water. The sky was a dreary grey; but cloudless, the rain stopped then the shimmering large moon glistened on the road side puddles.

I saw a light glowing close by and buildings, I kept my head down. The streets were desolated, I felt alienated; not welcome. A rambunctious laugh echoed in my ear but the streets were empty, what time even is it? What's the day? How long have I been walking?

As I carried on walking through the town, I came across a tavern; it was open. I walked in to see three old men talking to the tavern owner.

'Hello love, you're not from around here are you?' queried the owner.

'No I'm not, I just got here,' I replied.

'Make yourself at home. What can I get you?'

'Thanks, can I have a pint of beer?' I said, as I sat myself in a booth in the corner, the tattered old leather felt uncomfortable. I took off my soaked coat and plunked it on the floor.

'Ah, a man's drink, aha,' one of the old men said and winked at me.

Something didn't feel right here... I felt nervous, the old tavern owner came over and smiled while handing me my drink.

'Don't mind them old fools, they're drunk and they never leave,' he said, while rolling his eyes.

'Thank you, how much?' I ask.

'On the house, you look cold pet, you want a blanket?' he asked.

'Yes please, it was raining, thank you,' I reply.

I take a sip of my beer, the bitter taste filled my mouth. I don't even like beer that much, the taste made me scrunch my face. The old men looked at me.

'Eh you don't like it, I'll have it if you want?' one called over.

'You can if you want, it's not my type,' I called back.
One of the old men came over and sat down next to me and chuckled.

'What's a bonnie wee lass doing here?' he smiled.

'I don't know really, I'm Kate.'

'I'm George, that's Jim and John.' Two other men waved and smiled.
'That's the owner, Richard.'

'Do you know what time it is?' I asked George.

'Oi, Jim what's the time mate?' he called over to Jim who looked half asleep.

'Erm what *cough* oh right it's 11:37 mate.'

'Do you know where I can stay tonight?' I asked the four men.

I stood up with my dripping rucksack and flung it on my back.

'Stay here, I'm vacant, haven't seen any traveller in a longest of times, pet,' he insisted.

'Oh well, thanks, can I go to my room?' I asked.

'Sure, up the stairs on the left.'

I walked up the very creaky wooden stairs. The walls had pictures of fishing boats and old pictures of the tavern. I opened the door to my new place to stay for tonight, a double bed which looked so comfy and clean, the fire was on and the whole room was toasty. I took off my clothes and looked through the chest of drawers, searching for a nightie. A soft, dry flowery nightie was on top, I put it on and snuggled into the bed's duvet and pillows.

I was so tired I passed out within five minutes. The morning came around, I knew this because the sun blinded me through the pale yellow curtains of the small window. I stretched and opened my white painted door and peered round the door to see where the bathroom was; I spotted the bathroom and tip toed across to it. I scared myself when I saw Richard was standing there.

'Good morning,' I said.

'Hi Kate, I'll see you down stairs?' he asked.

'Yeah will do,' I replied.

I went back to my room and put my hair up in a messy bun and slid on some socks. I walked down the stairs to the bar and sat on a high stool.

'Hey, Kate, how would you like to work here because we need another bar worker and it gets really busy when the fishermen come back.'

Brat Camp
By Chelsea Scmalsteig

We're about to leave the house, to go to the airport and I've packed tonnes of clothes because my dad is being shady and secretive and won't even tell me where we're going, or how long we're going for! For all I know, we could just be going down the road to the old abandoned house and he could tie me up there and just leave...Wouldn't surprise me to be honest. I've always thought he was a bit of a psychopath.So, we've basically been driving for like 3 hours and we've said at least four words to each other, so it's kinda awkward here. Also we've passed the nearest airport and that airport is where they keep all the planes that take us to all the nearest countries in Europe. So if we actually are going to an airport it's probably going to be somewhere really far, so as you can imagine I'm obviously stressing out! I really wish my mum was here right now, because if she was here none of this would be happening. I cannot believe what is happening. No - this literally cannot be real life, how could my own 'father' be doing this to me? That psychopath is sending me to some 'Brat Boot Camp' in some place called Utah, where on this Earth even is Utah? This is absolute madness. I have been sat in the airport searching about this 'Brat Camp' and apparently it's something for troubled teens. There is no way in hell that I'm a 'troubled teen'. I've got friends worse than me and their parents haven't done this to them, and, apparently, "this is for my own good" and "he only has my best interests at heart", that's obviously a lie because if any parent cared about their child they wouldn't do this. I also have found out where Utah is, it's near the Nevada Desert. You know, the place with all the snakes, spiders and scorpions. Yep that's the one, and the place I'm going hasn't got these cute little snakes, ha-ha no, it has stuff like rattle snakes, the Black Widow , Desert Recluse and many, many more. This is outrageous. I'm probably not going to come back alive. Like how is this camp even real? How has it not been shut down yet? What if I get bitten by one of these terrifying beasts? This is literally my worst nightmare.

So, I board the plane in an hour, and once I finish my ten hour and nineteen minute flight to Utah, there is supposed to be someone picking me up from the airport and driving me to quite possibly the worst place on Earth. Also my 'Dad' is still here with me to make sure I don't run away. How pathetic, right? I don't know if I'm going to continue writing in this diary/journal once I get there, I suppose I can if and when I have time, but I doubt it.

2.6.14 Okay, so basically I've made it to Utah, sadly and it is obviously hot as hell because we're in the desert… and when I came off the plane and got my luggage there was a man and a woman waiting for me and they had my name on a sign so I knew who I had to go, and I'm not going to lie they looked absolutely terrifying, more so the man than the woman, and to add to this hell I'm in, the owners (the people who got me from the airport) of the camp are religious, but they aren't the type of religious people who keep their beliefs to themselves, Ohhhhh no. I've been here for less than two hours, and they've already started trying to push their religion upon me and it's not okay. One of their first few questions was "So, Ava, have you accepted Jesus as your Lord and saviour?' and the looks on their faces when I said 'absolutely not' was hilarious. After a few more minutes of them bombarding me with these religious questions I finally snapped and was like 'I'm sorry to break it to you, guys, but the clouds won't hear your prayers, If you want to sit there believing that there is someone sitting in the sky listening to you, then that's fine, but don't you dare try and force it upon me' and they just sat in the front of the car, all calm, and just giggled. I hate them so much, you'll never understand...But don't get me wrong, I don't hate or dislike people just because of their beliefs or whatever I just don't like it when they force it onto someone, it's not fair.

4.6.14 Sorry, I forgot to write in this journal yesterday, - there was basically no time and to be quite honest I literally could not be bothered. Nothing special happened yesterday, although I found out that the amount of clothes I had packed wasn't necessary because we have to wear this horrible uniform which is about the same colour as Shrek's swamp, and its long sleeves and long trousers, which are not ideal for this weather. I was also walked through the rules of this camp, obviously like no smoking or drinking, not that you can buy any here because there's no shop and we're in the middle of nowhere, but some of them are like 'Everyone has to be awake before 7 am,' 'all have to have breakfast,' 'you have to wear your uniform that looks like Shrek vomited on it, all day`, 'You have to be in bed before 10 pm every night,` and the best rule of this entire camp, is that 'everyone must attend church on Sundays!' Um no thanks… Also, you won't believe the beds we have to sleep on, they are bunk beds and the mattresses are so thin and uncomfortable, and we only get one pillow, which is not acceptable because I already have back ache from sleeping on that bed for just a night.

5.6.14 Okay, so it's about 12 pm. We got woken up by one of the camp workers here, by him shouting his lungs out, treating it as some sort of army. Its madness, I swear. Anyways, I dragged myself out of bed and into the shower. I soon found out that we only have ten minutes shower time. After I put on that dreadful uniform, I and Esme were sent into the assembly in the main hall, Oh, I forgot to mention, Esme is my friend here. She was sent here about the same time as me and we kind of just became friends. We're like the same people, basically. We like the same things, have the same sense of humour, I'm sure going to miss her when we get out of this place. Anyway the assembly was terrible (what a surprise), it was for all the new people here and they were just giving us information about the camp and how long we'll be here for and the punishments if we disobey the rules. To shorten it, basically, we're here at a camp in Utah in the middle of the dessert, it's called 'Brat Camp' and it's for troubled teens and they want to 'help' us sort our lives out, but at the moment it feels as if they're ruining mine. Also, we're here for a week and a half and to be quite honest, I don't think I can do it. The assembly wasn't like the normal ones you have in school either, you have to all stand there in silence in your Shrek coloured uniform and if you talk at all, this tiny 50 year old woman comes up barely reaching your face, and screams at you.

It's now 16:30 and I've just been let out of isolation I was put in there because I was talking to Esme and I got caught 'swearing', I'd hardly call 'Sh*t' a swear word though...anyway, in isolation I was forced to write a two page, (front and back,) essay type thing on why swearing is bad, and I also had to copy out all fifty absolutely mental rules at this hell and I wasn't allowed to leave unless I completed the 'task', so I ended up being in there for like two-three hours, and the room was so hot and humid because there was no air conditioning. I swear I was so close to death.

7:45 pm. We've just returned back from camp. The leaders decided to show everyone around the place where we currently are so we went walking around the desert and, of course, it would be me that ran out of water right at the beginning of the walk, so I obviously wasn't off to a good start. Also, the most terrifying experience I've ever been in was almost stepping on a rattlesnake! Well, I didn't so much actually step on the snake, actually it was like five-ten feet away from me, but, never the less, and it was terrible. I'm probably too traumatised to write for the rest of the night, so bye.

8.6.14 I don't know how many days I've missed out but I honestly couldn't care less because being thousands of miles away from my home, in some place I didn't know existed until a couple of days ago, is killing me. I'm home-sick, tired, bored and cannot get used to this climate, the people at this 'brat boot camp' say it gets better as the days go on, but it's just getting harder, I seriously cannot wait to get home. Also, I've been absent for the past two or three days because we've had to camp out in the wilderness for a while, we got given a little water to last for a couple hours and we also got given a tent for protection so we don't get killed by the wild beasts out here, and for the rest of the time we had to use the skills we were taught earlier on about how to make a fire or find more water, but, to be quite honest putting that tent up was a hard enough task on its own. But I have to admit it was really funny being out there watching everyone else struggle as well, we also had to eat these strange plants but we couldn't find many of them so me and Esme were hungry the entire time, Also there were some poisonous plants that looked similar to the ones we were looking for, so anytime we found a plant we were too scared to eat them but it was great also sleeping in that tent are the best night's sleep I've had since I've been here.

9.6.14 So, I've been for breakfast and lunch today and it was vile, it was some weird meat, I'm not quite sure what it was but I didn't enjoy it anyway, I found out that there are different stages to this boot camp and I'm in stage 1, the best one, because the higher the stages the more intense and strict the leaders and rules are, the higher the stage the worse behaved the people there are, so I'm actually quite pleased my dad decided to put me in this stage. I'm actually starting to quite miss him, to be honest, which is something I thought I'd never hear myself say. Also, tomorrow is my last day here, and it's a Sunday, which means Church, but you know what, I'm not going to make a big fuss out of it, I'm just going to go and get it over and done with and also a lot of the people here are religious so I don't want to offend anyone, but I won't be coming back to Church and suddenly become religious but it's only for a couple hours. I never thought being at this camp would 'change' me, well I never knew how bad my attitude was but just being away from my family has made me realise how much I took them for granted. There are some stuff I haven't written in here, like some of the stuff they made us do to knock some discipline into us but now I cannot wait to get home and show my family the new me, but I'm now going to stop writing before I get too emotional, I'm so lame haha.

10.6.14 it's my last day here today and I'll be leaving for the airport at 8 pm tonight. I'm not going to lie, even though I've complained every day I've written in this journal, it's honestly been one of the best and hardest experiences I've ever had and I'm so excited to go home and see my grandparents, dad and brother, although earlier on in week I did receive some news that my grandmother is back in hospital because she's had another heart attack. The doctors say they think she'll be okay but she's 87 years old so I'm so scared to see her in such a fragile state, but I know she'll be proud when she sees me. I didn't write any of this during the week because I was just trying to block it out of my head.

Esme and I have been spending time together today because we don't think we'll be seeing each other anytime soon, but we've been exchanging phone numbers and our Facebook names so we'll definitely stay in touch, I am going to miss her because she's the only person I've actually become friends with here, but we've promised each other that we'll visit one another in the future. The leaders have also allowed Esme to come to the airport with me so that's made me happy.

I went to Church as well today and it honestly was such a boring experience but I didn't make a fuss because it wasn't fair to the other people actually wanting to be there.

I've skipped many hours now because I've obviously been spending time with everyone else and I didn't want to be antisocial and just whip out my book and start writing. I'm currently on the plane and I've already started missing the place, it's true that even Hell can get comfy once you're settled in, but anyway I'm probably just going to go to sleep now because I've got another eight hours of flight, (how exciting,) so I'll probably write tomorrow.

11.6.14 I'm currently in the car going back home and I've never been so excited to see my dad in all my life and when I saw him everything between us was different. Different in a good way we are getting along really well he said I'm unrecognisable and I've definitely changed for the better, which I agree. This entire car journey has just been us talking about all the things that have happened while I've been gone, also what I've been going through on the other side of the world. It's been nice! The plan for, today, though is to go home, get something to eat, pick my brother up from school then go see my grandmother and words can't even describe how worried I am about seeing her.

It's much, much later now and unfortunately we didn't make it to the hospital in time, and my grandmother sadly passed away, and I'm so angry with myself because she didn't even get to see me now all she knows is me being a spoiled, bitchy, self-serving mess. This will forever be something I regret so much, but I and my family have been through this before and we're going to make it through, this even stronger than before.

Humanania
by Heather McCarthy

According to legend that has been passed down generations and generations of my family, the Human Race was free to do what they pleased on their planet, Earth. They were allowed to roam and go where ever they wanted; they were the top predators on the whole planet and were the most feared animals in the animal kingdom, or so they thought...

People think this 'freedom' era ended around the 21st century. The era when the human race was downgraded from predator to prey. The era when the new top predators arrived in the solar system, looking for something new to play with and control for their own selfish needs.

It is the year 3005, a millennium after those life changing events. Our story begins in Zone 15 (East United States). I'm walking home with my best friend, Lizzy. I've just turned eighteen last month but she's a few months older than me. I will be soon leaving school after I pass my CHS (Controlled Human Sciences). If I pass, I guess you could call me intelligent in a way, not trying to brag or anything! What always catches people's attention though, is my eyes. It's always the same thing: 'Your eyes are like Aqua sapphires! Or, 'Here comes our hero!' I ignore people who say that as it gets on my nerves! I don't believe in the legend that says that the Hero/heroine of the human race will have blue eyes; they have become extinct and no one knows why.

While I and Lizzy are walking back from school, we are talking about the recent reports about missing people from our zone. Lizzy seems to think it's the Aliens doing but I think it's just people trying to get away from the City. The Aliens have the most control on the Cities than the countryside as they aren't as spread out and it is easier to keep an eye on everyone. We say our goodbyes and I put my hand over the identification checker and walk into my gloomy house.

I wake up in a prison cell. I look around to see where I am, not much use. There is only a little a little square metal flap on what I am guessing is a door. I have to really concentrate but I realise I am not alone, I shout out, 'Hello?' And in reply, 'Is that you Az?!' It must be Lizzy! We must have been selected for The Games! It had to happen to me, didn't it? But then out of the millions of people they could have chosen to compete with me I get Lizzy. Well I guess that's the only upside of the situation.

It feels like hours that we have been alone in this horrible dark cell. All of a sudden, the door opened and a wave of light came flooding in. I was blinded for a few seconds while my eyes adjusted to it. Finally, I can see again and standing in the doorway is an Alien soldier. I have never seen one up close before but what an ugly sight! An expressionless face with two big circular eyes, no nose, a small mouth and a bald head. It's like staring at death in the face, literally! He orders us to get up and follow him without trying anything silly. We do what we are told and walk out of the cell behind him.

We are now waiting to start the game with the other contestants, in a line outside the Game Room's door. I and Lizzy have been selected to compete in The Electrifying Show, which is a game show what has four rounds and you have to answer as many questions correctly as you can to progress to the next round. The two people with the lowest amount of correct answers at the end of the round get electrocuted to death.

After ten minutes of waiting the doors open. I look at the piece of paper I have been given while waiting to enter to find out which seat I am in. Seat three next to Lizzy, luckily. We have to wait another five minutes for everyone to find and settle in their seats till the game starts. Some of the boys are excited to be chosen and eager to get on with it but there are a couple of girls who look nervous. Well, wouldn't you if you knew you were probably going to die and there is nothing you can do about it. Lizzy looks upset and has gone really quiet and me? Well you could say I'm not impressed about being here but I am naturally brave so I try my best in everything. The buzzer signals the game is about to start. I and Lizzy look at each other as to say 'To the end!'

The First Round is easy. I've got all my questions right and so has Lizzy. For each round all the questions are based on a certain subject e.g. Maths, T.V programs. This round is based on Human Sciences which is my favourite and best subject! But not everyone is good at it so one or two people have got a couple wrong. A pretty blonde girl and a small boy are the first to go.

The Second Round starts to catch people out. The subject is Maths, I don't really enjoy it but I wouldn't say I'm not good at it. Lizzy is ace at Maths so she's having no problems with it. I have only got one wrong so far which was a hard equation that involved Algebra. This round is designed to separate the intelligent people from, let's say, the not so clever people. I'm not trying to be nasty or anything it is true! The last two girls other than Lizzy are next to go.

The Third Round is the most important round I think because you have to fight for your place in the final round and for your life, even if it's not right to be forced to be a source of entertainment for a race of Aliens. This round the subject is T.V programs. Now I'm starting to get caught out as I hardly watch T.V - it bores me. Most of my questions are on soaps. Great, just great! When it comes to soap, I've no hope! Lizzy is doing ok but she is like me, she hardly watches T.V either. I think she is guessing most of her questions and luckily she is getting most of them right. However, I've got nearly all of mine wrong and we are on the last person till we move on to the next round. If this boy gets his question right I'm going to have to say goodbye to this cruel world. But YES! He's got it wrong! I might survive and be able to see daylight again one day.

Now I have to fight for my life against my own best friend, Lizzy! I know she doesn't want to do this but we have no choice; if we back out now we will both be killed on the spot so no one will get out of here alive. The Fourth Rounds subject is History, my worst subject possible. But Lizzy is currently studying Human History so it's working out for her. She has only got one wrong compared to my score, only two right and rest wrong. Now I'm definitely sure I'm going to lose my life. I'm no match against Lizzy in History and especially at this level. There is no point in even guessing now. But while Lizzy was about to answer one of her last questions, she quickly looked over at me and then on purpose she got the question wrong! I can't believe what I am seeing right now. Lizzy getting an answer wrong on purpose. It's really not like her at all! Then... ZAP!!! My best friend has just been turned into a pile of grey, smoking dust in a matter of seconds. I stay rooted to the spot, staring at the pile of dust that was the remainder of Lizzy's body. I don't know what to do. I have won my life back, I have won the game. I should be happy, jumping up and down in the air for joy. Only a selfish person would do that though...

I am going to be teleported back to my home Zone in a few hours to collect my things from my house. I have just received a letter from the Leader of the Aliens himself, passed on by a soldier. It says that I am being transferred to Zone 0 as my reward for winning the game. According to legend it is like a paradise, the world that is controlled by the Human Race, before the Alien race arrived, so you win back your rightful freedom.

The day has come that I move into this legendary Zone 0. I am still suffering with Lizzy's death and I will never be able to get the image of her being killed - blasted to dust and smoke - out of my head.

I've just been picked up and teleported to Zone 0's gates. The gates are made out of gold. They slowly open. I look straight ahead to see what my new paradise home is like. It's the complete opposite to a paradise! It's a farm and slaughter house. And I am… the meat!

The Goblin King
by Joshua Taylor

As the chest revealed its contents it was clear that whoever owned this chest was as rich as a king. Raganort could not believe his eyes, there were at least 1,000,000 gold coins. He had to go show it to the king because he would become a hero to all.

This dwarf was the king's nephew and he goes by the name Raganort. He was one of the best blacksmiths. Raganort had just been appointed captain of the Blood Ravens, which was the elite guard of the king himself, and the kingdom of Stone Forge. This was the smallest of the dwarf realms but by far the wealthiest, because of the vast amount of precious gems that were retrieved from mines. However, since the city has so many riches it spawned many enemies across the land.

There was one enemy whose name brought terror to even the bravest hearts, that name was Bone Crusher. He was the king of the goblins, and the vilest creature imaginable to man.

The king counted his gold every day, because he loved the treasure so much. Suddenly the dwarf king Glorin shouted "Quick the treasure has been taken!" Raganort rushed to his king's aid and the king called his council and they decided that Raganort would be the best at getting the gold. After that event the king took Raganort to one side and whispered in his ear. 'If there was any one else I could trust I would send them to get my treasure, but I only trust you, don't let me down.'

He set off for the castle at dawn because it would be a long and dangerous journey. Half way through this journey he was ambushed by a pack of goblins. He killed them in a second. On a body was a note saying they wanted him dead. He then realised how serious this mission was.

It was dark by the time he reached the castle. First he drew his bow and shot the gate keeper. He then hid in a coal cart as he travelled to the depths of the mine. As he got out of his hiding spot he realised Blood Crusher had many guards. There were twice as many as the Blood Ravens that were accompanying him. A guard walk past and he slit the goblin's throat. He then found his way to the main chamber of the goblin king. Bone Crusher was huge and smelt vile. However, there before him were the gems in an enormous chest. The goblin king roared, "Who dares show their face here?"
There was no reply.

The goblin king suddenly screamed with pain and then silence. Raganort had stabbed the goblin king in the heart and had felled his wickedness. He then opened the chest with a key he had found on the goblin king's body.

When he returned to Stone Forge there were great celebrations and he became Sir Raganort.

Murderer
by Kieron Marshall

After Latin Club I was walking down London Street toward the book shop when I saw a black van with black tinted windows. As it got closer towards me I had a sinking feeling something horrible was going to happen. I saw, from the corner of my eye, a man leaping out the van with some kind of object, and it wasn't a book! I tried to run but felt a heavy blunt blow smashing against the back of my head.

I woke up tied to a chair in a black room with a light shining down on me. I heard people talking in the background ... couldn't see them, though... as they got closer to me ... what they were going to do?! What have I done to them, to make them do this to me? I get bullied in college, and I was bullied back in school – just because I like to read and love to hang out in the library. Could it be that sadist, Joe Brindle, who always was a mean person to me, always getting his mates to bully me, just because I liked to read and went to Homework Club and got good grades. He couldn't spell to save his life – not even 'and'. He always tried to make his mates laugh, every time he saw me. Joe would always say this to me: 'Hey! Here comes the geek... chuck it a book!'

And I remember replying last time, 'At least I have a future. What about you, Brindle? Will you be working with your dad in the rubbish dump...?'

His mates had laughed and he hadn't liked that. I'd seen the evil stare he'd glared at me. So was it Brindle? Was that why I was chained up in darkness now?

Three days later... starving, thirsty, still locked up in some kind of cage. It is really dark. I can hardly see the floor. A figure is opening the cage door, maybe to let me out? I am really scared. What are they are going to do next? I feel weak, disorientated, about to faint. I am dying inside. As the figure opens the cage door I crawl backwards, trying to scurry away from him, but one giant fist grabs me. He drags me to the chair, then starts to whack and hit me with a giant, heavy book – so heavy it must be an encyclopaedia! He hits me on the legs with it and then the arms, and I think he is going to kill me by battering me to death with books. Then I hear a voice that sounds familiar floating through the nightmare and pain: 'You're the one who will be in the rubbish dump ... you'll be the one with no future, after I'm done with you, nerd...'

He raises the huge book high, ready to smash it down on my head and I feel terror in my face, darkness in my eyes... but then confusion... shouting.... flashing beams of torchlight... police are running in, the door banging, voices shouting. Brindle's brutal face pales with shock. He throws the book aside and starts to run away. The black figure gets dimmer ... smaller ... further away ... a black speck as small as a full-stop ... so far away that I cannot see him anymore.

My jailor and tormentor escaped. The police searched everywhere for him but not a sign. Brindle is gone. But I am free. Free again to continue with my studies. Free again to continue my quest and my reading and work my way to the top and rule the world. I will rule the world. There is no doubt about that. My tormentor might be free for now – but I'll track him down one day. Sooner or later. I will have my revenge. Because he knows – like everybody who is stupid really knows – it's geeks who rule, not bullies. It's geeks and nerds who really rule the world.

Burnt Ted
by Kelsey Eddington

The broken bear lay in the ashes and cinders of the fireplace, looking up through the chimney. Through glassy eyes he could see the stars. He wanted stars to be the last thing he looked at. Flames. He could feel the flames licking at his insides. He cried sawdust tears. He did not want to be burnt. If only he could get up and walk away – walk away backwards – into the past. He'd had a lovely owner, a sweet girl, and she'd loved him despite his disfigured face. From afar he could hear her crying and screaming at her parents. He could hear her footsteps clicking closer and closer. The next thing he knew he was dumped like a rag in a bucket of water.

Ted came round and saw the girl looking down at him, still crying. She lifted him out of the bucket and gently wrapped him in a towel. Her parents were out now. Elizabeth – the little girl – cuddled Ted close, rocking him gently. She was still crying, her tears dropping onto Ted's scarred face. She was still there, rocking him and weeping, when her parents came back. Her dad snatched Ted from her straight away. A row flared up. She started shrieking and wouldn't stop. She kicked; she shouted; she screamed and screamed. Ted was crying too, dust-tears spilling, knowing that his time was coming to an end – a time coming when he would never see Elizabeth again.

Elizabeth's mum sat beside her and cuddled her while she nodded at dad who was creeping off with Ted. He nodded back and slipped away into the kitchen, Ted gripped tightly in his strong hands. He didn't want the bear to escape again, not this time. Not after all they'd been through. In the kitchen bright glare he looked down at 'Burnt Ted' sorrowfully. A pathetic little teddy bear, burnt in some accident with a lamp he'd accidently been left leaning face-first against many years ago – burnt and scarred with a melted amber eye. An ugly bear. Just about as ugly as a teddy bear could be. Dad made the harsh decision. He opened the back door, pulled off the dustbin lid and dropped the ruin of Burnt Ted in, clanging the lid back on before he stepped back indoors.

In the stench of bin darkness Ted lay there, crying his burnt little eyes out. He lay there all night. The slow grey mist of dawn crept about the yard and dustbins. Through the dawn he heard the drone of a dustbin lorry approaching. He knew he had to get out of there or he would be history. He was pressed right below the steel bin lid. He tried to push it up but it only rattled and shuddered. He tried it again, pushing and shoving with all his teddy bear strength. He felt it give a little, and with one last mighty shove he managed to push the dustbin lid off and it clattered to the ground just as the heavy booted dustbin men came stomping into the yard. Burnt Ted managed to fling and roll himself to safety, rolling close to the back door. There was a cat flap in the bottom of the door, and as the bin was taken away to be emptied he managed to scuttle in through the flap.

Burnt Ted was furious. When he had been thrown into that dustbin something had snapped inside. Ted wanted to make Elizabeth's cruel and heartless father pay. After rolling through the cat-flap Ted crawled his way into the kitchen. He lay there in the middle of the floor, staring and waiting. Elizabeth's father came in at about 9 am, a lit match in his hand, lighting up his first cigarette of the day. Burnt Ted lay there, staring up, fury in his glass eyes. In shock, for he was not expecting Ted to be there or to be staring so fiercely, Elizabeth's dad threw the blazing match down onto Burnt Ted. Ted struggled up to his feet, burning and blazing – the match had caught in his stuffing and set him on fire again. He looked up, giving his cold and hard glassy stare. Elizabeth's father tried to run away but he could not pull himself from the glassy stare of the blazing teddy bear. Burnt Ted rushed forward, wrapping his little stumpy arms about his tormentor's lower leg. The pyjamas were nylon. The flames soon spread.

'I will come back for my revenge and that's a promise,' hissed Burnt Ted. 'I warned you I'd be back...' Elizabeth's dad was screaming and trying to shake the blazing teddy bear off but it gripped harder and harder onto his calf muscle.

'Ashes to ashes and dust to dust... ' Burnt Ted cried out as he clutched tight and the flames flared higher '... if the Devil don't get you, then Burnt Ted must!'

The fire was fierce and devastating. Elizabeth and her mother were lucky and managed to escape. But of dad... nothing was ever found, not even ashes. And of Burnt Ted? All that remained was a single, staring amber bead of melted eye.

The Fairground
by Aurora Lindley

It was a misty night on the 31st October 2014 (also known as Hallowe'en). Looking from my window, I could see in the distance the trees roaring in the wind and kids in various costumes struggling to battle through the massive gusts of wind.

I was in my bed room, waiting for all my friends, because we were going trick or treating. Joey is the mysterious one; he is very quiet until you get to know him and you never know what he is thinking. Ryan, who is known as the loud and annoying one, always trying to get on your nerves. Ollie is constantly silly; he is always coming up with stupid jokes, trying to make everyone laugh. Jordi is as handsome as a Hollywood film star, and boy does he know it! Andy, the best out of all of us; he has been adopted by several people in the past and so I haven't known him for that long but he always puts others before himself. As for me, I'm Bailey, I guess I'm the leader but only because I organise everything and if I didn't nothing would happen.

'Knock knock, they're here!' my mum yelled, as I rushed down the stairs and clambered out the door. Before I knew it, we were stumbling past the foggy park at the end of my street, when Jordi noticed a dark alley way in the distance. We had never noticed it before.

'I don't think we should go down there, it doesn't look safe and have you seen the poster that is near the shop? It's about an alley way and at the other side there is a terrifying clown that is trying to capture people...' Ollie alleged.

'Oh shut up, Ollie, don't be silly, it's a load of rubbish,' declared Joey.

However, before we knew it, Jordi and Ryan were running down the hazy alley way and promptly disappeared in the foggy mist.

The rest of us tried running after them but they were gone - we couldn't see them anywhere. We carried on walking warily and as we got to the end of the alley, Joey noticed an abandoned fairground. We pondered over to it, everything was still. There was no one around. It was silent. Jordi and Ryan were still nowhere to be seen and we were getting increasingly worried about them.

'I think we should just go back now,' I said, but they all disagreed with me.

Ollie ran over to the waltzers so we all followed him. The fairground was so big we didn't know where to start looking for them. It was dark and we could hardly see a thing. We were walking round and suddenly I heard a noise; frightening music started playing, there were flashing lights and the fairground rides turned on. I heard a scream, I spun around. Joey had disappeared. I could see Ollie and Andy in front of me so I tried running up to them but it was too late; All I could see was loads of fairground rides somewhere completely black and not moving but others had lights on, I had lost them all and I was on my own, alone...

I stopped and stood there, looking at the floor, I didn't know where I was, All I knew was that I was standing in the middle of a fairground, on my own. Suddenly, I heard large footsteps coming towards me. I looked up and there was a clown stumbling towards me; he was wearing enormous red pointy shoes, long striped trousers, he looked very angry and his face was all white with two enormous red circles on his cheeks, he had a big red curly afro. I started to run but my conscience pulled me back, where were my friends? I couldn't leave without them, without knowing where they were. It was only then that it occurred to me that maybe I was the brunt of a trick; people don't just randomly disappear..!

'Ryan is that you? You're not scaring me,' I shouted as I spun around. Doubt crept into my mind when I realised that the clown was at least a foot taller than any of my friends. I felt like I was stuck, I didn't know what to do, I wanted to leave, to run and not turn back, but what about my friends? And who was this in front of me? My mind was racing.

'Andy, where are you?' My voice echoed round the fairground... there was no reply. Then I became aware that the clown had a yellow juggling club in his hand above his head, I screamed as it came hurtling towards me and then everything went black...

I woke to a strange vision of myself; it was me but somehow different. My head was throbbing, I felt queasy, I rubbed my eyes, I slowly realised that I was in the hall of mirrors, the strange vision was a reflection of myself in a curvy mirror. I tried to stand up but my hands were fastened behind my back. I looked around and I saw Ryan, Jordi, Ollie and Andy but not Joey; I couldn't see Joey anywhere.

'I can't stand up!' I yelled. At that moment the clown stumbled into the room, tripped over the ridiculous shoes, his wig and mask skidded across the room to reveal ... Joey.

'Joey, what are you doing?' we all shrieked.

'It wasn't me honestly, that man; he forced me to put the clown costume on and then decided to push me in here so I would get the blame for tying you up when it was him!' Joey cried. Joey took the rest of the clown costume off and came to help us all, one by one.

'WATCH OUT,' Jordi bellowed as I rotated round to see the man who was running towards me, he had dark skin with long lanky legs and a black curly beard. We all ran towards the door.

'Follow me, I know the way out,' I shrieked.

We all carried on running and the man carried on running, too, we could finally see the beginning of the alley. I turned and it looked like the man was running but he wasn't moving, it was as if there was a big glass window in front of him that he couldn't get past. I looked to see the other boys but they were all completely gone and I was outside my house...

Attack on Titan: Defence of the HQ by Laura Gibson

Mikasa advanced forward over the grey tiled roof top, a bead of sweat trickled down her forehead. Her breathing increasing every minute, she glanced briefly over her shoulder. The 4 metre sized titans she had previously seen must have lost track of her. She slowed to a stop, sighed and collapsed into an exhausted pile…

Her name is Mikasa Ackermann, an elite soldier for squadron 104, team 36, her skills were outstanding. But she had a twisted drive to kill; she had watched her parents die, by being axed to death, their attackers were unknown, but what she had seen lead to her willpower to kill titans.

Mikasa rose up and straightened her scarf before spotting a 15 foot titan. She yanked out her blades and pulled on the trigger to activate the 3D manoeuvre gear, it would run off gas which were attached to the back of the blade holders and would spring out two thin wire lines to grapple onto building, trees etc. to be out of the hand of titans. She blasted forward, blades ready, grappled onto the back of the titans' nape, their only weak spot. She skilfully sliced out a large chunk of the abominations neck then pressed the triggers to pull herself onto the building opposite. She landed gracefully, turned on her heels and observed the titan plunge to the ground that was her 24th kill today.

Since the titans have breached the city everyone has had to evacuate. Leaving trainee corps, soldiers and scouts and military police to kill the large, unknown monstrosities. Mikasa made out a familiar voice, it was Armin, another elite for squadron 104.

'Titans have endeared headquarters and are trapping the supply team inside, no supply team means no gas, which means we're dead...this could be bad.' He positioned himself next to her then glanced down at the decomposing, steaming titan body. 'Nice work.' He stated.

'Thanks, How many dead and how many casualties?' She replied, a hint of worry ran through her voice. '204 dead,372casualties.'

'Call over squad 104 and all teams within it... Then tell them to fight off the titans on HQ.'

'Will do.' He was off like a gust of wind zooming over rooftops.

'Don't die...' Just as she replied he was gone.

Mikasa squinted her eyes to see, in the distance, titans climbing on HQ. She grunted angrily and set off towards HQ. As she passed, she saw bodies, well her comrades dead, or being eaten by fowl titans, limbs scattered, blood splatters everywhere. 'You didn't die in vain, humanity will rise again,' she whispered to herself.

Armin and 37 other elites started taking down titans, one by one. Slicing their napes, blinding the more challenging ones, then destroying them. Armin glimpsed over his shoulder to see Mikasa and joined her in killing another monster. After 20 minutes of killings HQ was free of titans, there were 15 deaths out of 39, 2 casualties but everyone in the supply team was unharmed.

The remaining soldiers restocked their gas tanks and headed back to Wall Maria to confirm their victory against titans for today.

We Were Soldiers
by Mark Hall

This is a page thought to be from an artefact written by the famous Roman hero, Julius Hillier, who was thought to have lived in the region of Dalmatia, in the first century AD. It was found among the ruins of a Spartan prison camp on the coast of Greece.

*

As my crew and I continued on our voyage to Anatolia, we knew there was something here with us, and I don't mean the prisoners. We sensed an unusual presence from the sea. When I looked into the glistening sea, I felt as if something was watching me. I rapidly turned around, to see nothing but a splash. Even I was scared at first, over the days it became a familiar presence, and it always seemed to be accompanied by a distant tune that reminded me of my wife. However, I could see that it scared my crew. Everybody was praying to Neptune for mercy, the slaves were rioting like monkeys. Kierolius the hardest man on the ship was even a bit jumpy, that says something. I don't know what to do. I could turn back but Emperor Nero would kill us all! Most of my men had families so I couldn't do that.

All of a sudden we heard chanting coming from a pile of rocks! I have never seen anything so beautiful to this day. It was a beautiful, blonde girl with the face/voice of an angel. My crew and I are dazed by her, but old Billius (the ship's lookout) didn't fall for her venomous trick. He explained that she was many of the evil *Hierro* creatures. They lure their prey with their beauty then they strike. They aim for the keel of the ship with tremendous power, piercing it with their sharp, razor teeth. These creatures attacked ships for fun. They attacked anyone. Big or small, they could wipe out anything in these seas.

That's exactly what she did. Our ship was wrecked! We were lucky to be close to land, but it was Greek land. We could tell because the town near us had a big Greek symbol in the town centre. We had to make our way to neutral land to send out a smoke signal for help…

If I Wake Up
by Poppy Williams

When the tea party began, the same sinister music also began to play. It seemed to last hours and hours before the innocence faded away, and the room started to spin... The same music sped up to a pounding pace, and before I knew that the routine had started and I was being sent to Hell. I started to run, no sprint, as the time seemed to increase in speed; the chase of a lifetime began. The eerie music, which surrounded me, seemed to penetrate my ear drums. Faster! Louder! The chase seemingly lasted hours and hours; however it never slowed down at all. Screaming for help this time would be pointless, I have learnt that many times before. Nevertheless, the menacing sounds still tortured me, nobody could save me. Even if I stopped running, the horror would carry on. Laughter screeched from behind me, creeping closer and closer, faster! The air became heavy, just as it always did, the air felt as though it was filling with rocks, surrounding me and captivating me. My lungs felt as though they were deflating and closing up. To follow the routine, my vision was slowing but surely fading away...

The monstrous figure behind me yelled words out that I knew I didn't understand, another language that made me feel physically sick. The volume vibrated through my entire body, the words seemed to be destroying my brain. The word laughter these days scares me out of my skin, just hearing it sends the satanic signals to my brain. When I get to the point when I begin to tire, I feel the claws sink into my skin, and then it all simply ends; all the long lasting terror which scares me through the nights, ended.

I awoke in a wet and soggy state, the sweat soaked my hair, and my bed sheets were coated in a layer of urine. I sighed. My mother also likes to follow a routine, she loves to raise her voice, and bellow down the house, 'Candice why must you be so selfish! Do you not realise by now that I have to slave away every single day just because you can't go to the bloody toilet before bed?' I shrugged. I know for myself that I can't help it, but Mother doesn't, and yet again, I have disappointed her.

My mother ran around the house, chasing my younger brother and eventually successfully forcing him into his shabby school uniform. She told me every morning that she would soon get on to talking to me, however she never did, she would always focus on my brother, Nick, until the time came to go to school. The walks to school were never smooth and easy either; they always involved kicking, screaming and whining from Nick. The only person he ever listened to was my father. I rarely was allowed to go out onto the street and be with the other kids my age, my mother told me that the world was dangerous and I should try and stay indoors for protection, and I believed her.

Arriving home was quite terrifying for me, as I knew that, soon, I would have to get into bed again, and go to sleep. In the meantime, I always tried to occupy myself. Mother helped me with that. She would have me wash the dishes, make all the beds, wipe down the surfaces and, later on, tackle the task of putting Nick to bed. This was definitely the hardest of my tasks. He listened to me even less than he listened to Mother, and she would just ignore me if I was to ask for any help. These were the jobs my Father used to do. By the time I had finally put Nick to sleep, it was time for me to go to sleep myself; the time I feared the most.

Mother would come stomping into my bedroom, and would remind me of my punishment if I failed to keep a clean bed. That frightened me even more; I began to feel as though I was trapped in my own home, unable to escape the nightmare. Even though knew I was strong, tears fell from my eyes, and onto my pillow. This would make Mother angry. She believes that crying is for the ungrateful, and I should realise how lucky I am, but I can't help it. The night was, again, long and fearful, the same nightmare was following me, and I didn't know what I did wrong to deserve it. Mother always told me to believe that I'm only ever being punished for doing bad things. So I know I must have done something to deserve the dreams. Maybe I'm the reason I no longer really have a father, and now I'm being punished.

When the weekends rolled around, I was still told to remain indoors, no matter how nice the weather outside was, how peaceful the traffic was or how nice the neighbours were, I was trapped indoors, helping Mother with the housework, and, 'staying out of the way'. I never had the option to do much other than clean, as Mother told me to respect her for all she did for me, which I accepted. People told my mother that my brother was struggling with mental issues, but she just dismissed it.

Three years of boredom, suffering and nightmares and it was finally my 11th birthday, and Mother was starting to open up to the idea of letting me go outside with other children, and Nick was becoming for stable too. Last year, Mother decided to go to a therapist to seek help for caring for children for the most part it worked, although she still often left me alone for hours… As a celebration for my 11th birthday, Mother decided to take Nick and I somewhere, which we were both quite frankly ecstatic about. However, Nick was now at the age of 5, and he enjoyed running around, and disobeying Mother, which often made her quite angry and led to her taking her anger out on me.

Mother, Nick and I set out for the fair which had pitched up in town, my excitement was overflowing, but I could see that Mother was growing impatient with Nick. He shot down paths, stumbled into people and caused a scene when Mother decided it was enough. In my attempt to shut out the dysfunctions of my family, I gazed hopefully at the bright lights above me, I felt as though they were watching me, telling me it would turn out okay... However this was hard to believe. I began to wonder if what I was doing was right, or whether I could do something more to help Mother and Nick, maybe I could redeem myself for what I did to my father...

The atmosphere seemed to become gradually more enjoyable, Mother somehow became a completely different person, and she was accepting and happy. She didn't shout or make a scene; she managed to keep everything under control, despite her treating me like a 5 year old. But it was okay, because nobody looked at us as if Nick had problems, and looked at Mother with shameful eyes. I was having fun, which was a strange feeling, but it made me feel warm, and loved. Nick went on rides, and Mother even offered me candyfloss and I felt as if my life was finally changing for the better, and that Mother was opening up to the idea of forgetting. She laughed, she had a bounce to her walk, and it was as if she was forgetting everything that happened to her, as I was too. As the auburn-buttercup sun fell from the sky into the dark night.

We all got onto the 'flying saucers' Mother smiled at me, my stomach jumped, but not in the fearing way it had previously, I think she was happy to be with Nick and I. As we sat through the two minute ride, Nick squealed as it went faster, Mother squeezed us tighter 'be careful not to slip out, Candice!' Mother yelled at me over the loud, jolly music of the ride. Mother's change in personality was what I had been dreaming of for years, what I thought my life would have turned out if father had stayed.

Nick finally grew tired after hours of wandering, and Mother declared it was time to go home. But I didn't want to anymore I wanted to stay here always, completely hypnotised by the luminous lights twinkling above me and I gazed at them, I felt warm, almost comfortable and content. I turned quickly, suddenly feeling as though my stomach had dropped, my palms became clammy… Mother and Nick, where are they? Cold water flushed onto my feet and sent shivers up though my body and I felt bursts of panic popping in my brain. Alone. Trapped. I closed my eyes, and tried to thing rationally. Mother wouldn't leave me, would she? Maybe she'd planned this… Was it even possible to abandon your child and simply never come back? The magic of the fun fair was coming to a sudden halt.

Air was becoming tighter, as if somebody was sucking the air from my lungs as I breathed. My vision was becoming distorted. I felt as though I was phased into my nightmare, the sweat coming from my forehead seemingly in gushes, felt realer than ever, as though I was really drowning... Maybe *it* will come after me too... I hastily span around in an attempt to search for the thing destroying my happiness which I thought I had finally obtained. The twinkling lights around me transformed into demonic glowing eyes, targeting me, to hunt me, the fair music surrounding me converted into the familiar noise I had been hearing for the past three years.

The monsters surrounding me huddled in closer, throwing their claws at my body and screaming nonsense into my ears. There is nowhere to run, nowhere for them to chase me to, and nowhere for me to hide. I hear Mother's angry screams from the crowd too, but where is she? Why can't I see her? For the first time, I feel like I need to cry for help or nothing will change, but when I open my mouth to shout, nothing comes out. Tears stream out of my face and the world around me starts to spin, just like it has done for the past three years. If this is just a nightmare, I will wake up soon, I just need to survive the night, or I need someone to wake me up. I hear my name drifting further and further away from me, 'Candice! Candice!' The world stopped spinning and the monsters fade away into the darkness, my breathing slows down, my eyes shut, and there are no longer demonic eyes around me, no suffering, and no fear. Nothing.

The Machine
by Tom Noble

Duncan could feel the rain soaking through his thin, worn hoodie as he dribbled the basket ball up the court. The battered ball was at risk of bursting into a cloud of rubber, with every bounce on the tarmac, due to its extreme usage - despite the extensive amount of care and attention Duncan gave it. The rough fabric of his hoodie began to rub the water against his toned skin, turning it a light shade of red and purple. The ball continued hopping back up to Duncan's hand until he finally grasped it with both hands and leaped up, as graceful as a lioness and as fast as a cheetah. He extended his arms out down toward the hoop and brought the ball crashing down.

Duncan remained hanging on the hoop, swinging in the torrential rain above the concrete. He knew he had to drop eventually and return to his miserable life, but he just hung there, listening to the soft pattering of the rain on the ground and the smooth rustle of leaves. He noticed the parts of railing that were sharp from being cut by vandals. *Loras Park's Basketball Court, all hoping to keep their hands stay out* he thought with a smirk. He loosened his grip and fell to the ground, scooped up his ball and walked out of the court with a sigh.

The rain eased off as he turned upon the street where his house was located, and the sun shone down ironically on his joke of a home. The white paint was peeling to show the plaster beneath and the windowsills were hanging from their intended spots. Duncan eased the door open silently and flopped down onto the sofa-bed by the kitchenette. Dust consumed the air around him, rising from the archaic furniture. The room was still and void of life. *Where is Sophie?* He thought as he spotted Sophie's plastic chair, facing the ancient TV, empty. He stood up and moved around the small room slowly, swatting away bugs as he did so. In a feeble attempt to swat away a crazed fly that insisted on following him, he hit the bulb hanging from the ceiling sending a layer of dust down on him.

Duncan coughed and was about to sit himself down again when he heard a faint whimper escape from one of the cupboards in the kitchenette. *Rats again,* he thought to himself, and he grabbed a pan hanging above the stove. He drifted over to the cupboard and yanked it open with one quick tug. 'Dunky!' his sister leapt out of the cupboard into his arms.

'What were you doing in there silly?' Duncan replied, ruffling her blonde curls.
'I was looking for food... Mommy is in the bathroom with the needles again...' Duncan sighed and shot a glance to the bathroom.
'C'mon Soph, lets get you something to eat', Duncan began scouring the empty cupboards unsuccessfully before finally finding a year old can of spam. 'The food of kings,' Duncan laughed with his sister.

They were just sitting down to their elegant meal of fried spam and lukewarm water when their mother burst from the bathroom exuding a feeling of sickness and nausea into the room. She staggered over to the table and slammed her fists down onto it. 'Where have you been all day? I was here, trying to take care of your sister, and you were out playing with that stupid ball!' She had gotten up in his face during her rant and the smell of old cigarettes drifted up his nose.

'If locking yourself in the bathroom, shooting up and not feeding your daughter is considered 'taking care', then you deserve an award!'
She dropped her gaze to the ground. 'I was just taking a break,' she muttered as she dropped into an empty seat beside Sophie.

'You need to get it together; we are all suffering because of your habits, Mom... if I can even call you that.'

She paused for a moment, staring blankly at the ground, then an angry sneer grew across her face. Her right hand balled into a fist and she flung it at Duncan. It connected with his nose with a sharp snapping sound. 'How dare you insult me like that! I feed you and clothe you alone and this is the respect I get?' She was leaning over him, spit spluttering out of her mouth as she bellowed.

Duncan could taste something metallic and sprung to his feet, his whole body flooding with rage. 'It isn't our fault that Dad decided to bail on us! He didn't want to leave but I'm sure anyone would have in his position; you were awful to him, Ma... All he wanted was to be a good dad and husband, but you made that impossible for him.' She had backed away slightly, and refused to keep eye contact with him 'You are the reason we are in this mess, not us, yo-' Before he could finish, his mother's fist was in his face again and he could feel the coldness of the tiles beneath his head. He lay still for a few seconds, trying to suppress the extreme pain he felt in his face and nose. This was the first time his mother had lashed out at him and he had begun to realise the seriousness of the situation; his mother was dangerous and he and his sister were trapped there with her – like flies in the web of a spider. He and his sister had to get out, or they would likely perish to the hands of their own mother.

Duncan eased himself up off the floor and heard his sister crying from under the table. He leaned down to look at her.

    'It's okay now Soph, I think she went out. Let's eat our food then get some sleep.' She took her head out of her hands and crawled over to him, embracing him tightly. 'Don't worry Sophie, it's all gonna be okay.' Duncan stroked the stray blonde lock that always fell over her eyes, but he knew more than anyone that it wasn't.

*

Duncan awoke before his sister and pushed himself off the sofa. As he moved into the bathroom the awful stench of his mother's drug abuse was still strongly evident and empty syringes and cigarette butts littered the floor. He tangoed across the room, dodging the debris, towards the mirror, and groaned at the sight of himself. Duncan was usually a very handsome boy, however the irrational actions of the night before had transformed his face, leaving it black and bruised and his broken nose disrupting the good looking symmetry.

He pulled on some shorts and a t-shirt, grabbed his ball and headed out. The morning air was refreshing and there was little movement on the streets. Duncan finally had some peace as he made his way to Loras Park. Duncan noticed a flyer pinned to a board as he walked into the park, it read: *'Do you think you could be the next sporting legend? Do you think you have what it takes to be the best? Now is your opportunity! Our sporting agents are looking for the hottest new talent from all around the country -'* Duncan filled with hope and a grin spread across his face. *'- for a range of different sports, these include: Soccer, ice hockey, football, basketball, volleyball, baseball and dodgeball. Come on over to NYC -'*

Duncan's hope had begun to fade away but he pocketed the flyer anyway. *Could I raise enough money to get to New York?* he thought. *And I couldn't leave Sophie with Mom, the agents may not even think I'm good enough… No, I have to hope.*

Walking up the path through the park to the court, Duncan admired the beauty of the place. Despite the kind of people that lived in the surrounding neighbourhoods the scenery of the park was still an exquisite display; the leaves of the trees shone a dazzling emerald green in the golden rays of the sun, and beautiful carvings were etched into the pathway that circumvented the park.

With the fizzle of hope still fresh in Duncan's mind, he was ready to get started, and he let the ball bounce to the ground as soon as he entered the court. He practised his long range jump shots, successfully scoring 90% of them, before continuing onto his special and favourite move; the dunk. After a strong first dunk, Duncan kneeled down to pick his ball when a familiar voice came from behind him.

    'Guys, look, it's Michael Jordan! Oh no, wait, it's just a lanky white kid who *thinks* he's Michael Jordan.' As if the laughter that erupted around the voice was his cue, Duncan spun around to see Jackson with his 'gang' stood around him. He was a tall African-American boy, packed from head to toe in heavy muscle, and he wore low hanging cargo shorts and a ripped hoodie. But it was his face that tended to scare most; he constantly wore a dominant looking scowl which seemed to be the reason why he was the leader of his pack of troglodytes.

    'Not now, Jackson… Just leave me alone and I'll practise in this half of the court,' Duncan replied, his hands shaking as they awkwardly played with the ball in his hands.

'Oh, would you look at that,' Jackson ignored pointing, at Duncan's face. 'Pretty boy not so pretty anymore. What happened white boy? Momma beat you again?' The rest of the group laughed robotically as they re-enacted Duncan being hit by his mother. 'C'mon Duncan! You're supposedly the man of the house after your wimp of a -' Duncan felt his body temperature rise and he saw red before thrusting his body towards Jackson.

'Do not talk about my father like that!' The words poured out of his mouth and he realised Jackson was wincing ever so slightly; Duncan couldn't remember doing it but his fist was now raised in the air, pointing down towards Jackson.

'Hey, hey, hey! Ease up, bro! You wanna try thinking about what you're doing muchacho or Imma' knock your teeth out!' One of Jackson's squad had stepped in between them. Duncan lowered his fist and tried to calm himself. He wouldn't sink to their level.

'Okay, Wilt Chamberlain,' Jackson mocked. 'you want the court? Then I'll play you for it, one on one.' Duncan looked down at the ground, *I know I can beat him, I know it,* he told himself silently *but what will he do if I win? I doubt he will be as honourable as he says...* Duncan was unsure what to do, the clock was ticking but the dilemma was whirling in his mind. 'Well, what's it gonna be?' Jackson sniggered.

'I'll do it,' Duncan blurted out in a rush of confidence and pride. The smirks on the faces of the people in the crowd were replaced with those of
shock, and they all turned to Jackson to hear his retort.

Jackson paused for a moment, before leaning in close to Duncan 'You got too much pride and not enough sense.' he then turned without a response and walked over to the worn bench to collect his much more suitable ball. Duncan tossed his to the side and turned to face Jackson. Duncan was starting to feel doubt and regret, but before he could process all of his emotions, the match had begun…

The Mexican boy that had spoken up earlier took the ball 'Okay, chicos, first to ten shots wins, or the person with the highest amount of shots before the buzzer, which will be ten minutes. You both know the rules, let's do this!' With that brief introduction, he hurled the ball up into the air. Duncan bent his knees ever so slightly and propelled himself up into the air, pushing the ball slightly his way with his fingertips. They were playing just with one net, so Duncan swiftly pivoted on his right leg and dribbled the ball towards the net. With his incredible speed he gave Jackson no chance to take lead and defend, and quickly scored with a lay-up shot.

Jackson did nothing to hide the disappointment and anger welling up inside of him. He started advancing towards Duncan, but the Mexican boy who seemed to have taken on the position of the official, stopped him 'Ey, ey, ey, gabacho, chill! Settle this with the ball, not your fist.' Jackson glared at him for several moments through his menacing eyes, eventually moving back to face Duncan, readying himself for the jump ball. The ball was thrown and the game resumed…

Successfully blocking a shot, Duncan pivoted around and proceeded with great pace towards the net. It was 9-9 with one minute to go; it would probably go to sudden death if no winner was crowned. Large beads of sweat crawled down Duncan's gleaming arms and legs as he manoeuvred his way around the court, thinking carefully about every move he took. Duncan was doing everything possible to try and gain headway, but Jackson had moved in front of him and was putting all his power into defence; he was very clearly fine with it being a draw, but would never let Duncan humiliate him in front of his friends by winning. Noticing this, Duncan knew what he had to do. He began moving from side to side at high speeds, bringing Jackson along with him. He wound his way around the court, pushing Jackson slightly away with his back. Duncan noticed Jackson's breathing intensifying, and the arc created with his arms over Duncan's head was getting lower… It was working!

Duncan quickly moved to his left again, Jackson now following more slowly. '30 seconds!' The Mexican boy called out from the benches. Duncan had to act now or the game would end a draw. For a split second, Duncan noticed Jackson slip slightly and he saw his chance, he thrust his whole body to the right and twirled around Jackson. The net was in his sight and a clear path led toward it. Duncan shifted into full speed and bolted towards the net, shouts and cries coming from behind him. His whole body was working like a machine, all the individual parts and cogs working in time, together, doing precisely what they were intended to do. Duncan felt like a separate entity, watching over his body at the magnificence of his skill; and it was within this moment than Duncan knew this was what he was destined to do, he was destined to be one of the greats, one of the legendary all stars.

Before he knew it, Duncan's whole body had risen off the ground and the ball was slamming down from his hands into the net. 'TIME!' the kid shouted just as the ball whipped through onto the ground. He had done it; he had won *and* performed a buzzer beater. Duncan couldn't help the huge grin that was forming across his face, he did nothing to hide it, and why should he? He had performed excellently and he felt more proud than ever before.

He paused for a moment and realised how much he had pushed his body; as he stood up he felt a sharp twang of pain at the bottom of his spine. He reeled his body around to see the crowd gawking at him, their jaws dropped. The Mexican boy stepped up beside Jackson and uttered, 'Damn Jackson, you can't say this muchacho hasn't got skill.' Jackson's scowl grew more intense and he turned to face the boy.

'What did you just say to me?' Jackson whispered, making the Mexican boy step back slightly. Jackson's hands had shifted into fists and the Mexican boy's eyes darted wildly around his friends; looking for the assistance that never came.

'Uh, it's just… you can't deny that he's go-' His words were cut off sharply by Jackson's fist smashing into the side his face. His whole body crumpled to the ground, and Jackson spun and darted towards Duncan, his eyes roaring with rage.

He clutched Duncan by his collar and glared at him, his hand held back ready to strike. 'How dare you do that to me?! You should know by now how this works, you lose and I win. I own you boy, I will never let you forget this.' In the fury of those words Duncan did not hear Jackson speaking. He was merely a projection of his mother, and the built up rage within him was threatening release.

Duncan winced as he saw the fist fly towards his face, and then his vision went black. He tried to open his eyes but all he saw was the world spinning around him, getting lighter and darker, closer and further away as he slid in and out of consciousness. He could feel a falling sensation, and then something very hard hitting the back of his head. He watched as the tall boy loomed over him, staring down through those hate filled eyes. His vision began to turn black again, and with a smirk on his face, he let the darkness consume him.

Sometime later, a distant snapping sound came from around him. It began to get louder and louder until it was right in his ear. Then a voice boomed, 'Yo dude, he messed you up bad! I thought I got something awful but jeez... I was wrong, gabacho.' Duncan snapped open his eyes to see the other target of Jackson's abuse staring back down at him.

'Ahhh there he is. Rise and shine, big guy!'

'Ach, what happened? Where did Jackson go?' Duncan said as he slowly sat upward, all his joints and muscles aching with every move. The other boy's eyes shifted away, and his smile faded.

'Oh that guy... well he clocked me and then clocked you, idiota. I think you may have a mild concussion,' he joked, helping Duncan return to his feet. Duncan wobbled a bit at first but soon found his balance. 'I'm not a doctor or anything, but I think he put your nose back right...' Duncan lifted his hand to his nose and to his surprise he was right! His nose was now firmly back in the centre of his face; even if it did still throb with pain.

Duncan looked around the court and smiled, he knew that despite the beating he had taken, he would always remember this place with fondness not matter how far he got in his career.

'Never liked that pinchazo anyway, walking around this place like he owns it. Heh, he got what he deserved in the end.'

Duncan turned to what seemed to be his new friend 'Wait what? What happened to him?' He asked, secretly hoping he'd been hit by a bus. The other boy let out a chuckle and gestured him to sit on one of the benche.

'After he beat down your puny culo, the gang started shouting at him about honour and what not, and in the end they ended up kicking him out. He tried to resist so they beat that muchacho to a pulp,' A grin formed on both of their faces. 'He ended up limping home crying for his mommy.' He sighed through bursts of laughter.

As they sat there on that bench in Loras Park, Duncan could feel the incunabula of a friendship. A friendship where Duncan never thought possible, one that would grow and last a lifetime. Duncan finally felt compatible with someone for once in his life, finally felt safe and secure, and best of all, happy. 'Dude, what's your name?' Duncan asked through his grin.

'Arturo, Arturo Mendez nice to meet you,' he mocked in a posh accent, and despite already knowing the answer, he asked politely 'What about you, homie?'
And for once, in all of the seventeen years he had been muttering his surname or speaking of it only in shame, he said

proudly and confidently in the same mocking tone 'Duncan, Duncan Smith.'

After parting ways with his new companion, Duncan couldn't keep his mind racing from the events of the night. Arturo had informed him that he was out cold for at least two hours, which made their friendship even stronger, knowing that he had waited for so long. They ended up conversing and showing each other their basketball specialties, until the sunlight was swapped with the moonlight, and the goldfinches swapped with owls. Finally, at 11:30, they decided it best to go home, they traded addresses and walked out of the court. They met as enemies, and parted good friends.

As soon as Duncan walked through the door, his mother was clutching him, weeping and shouting things incomprehensible.

'Mom, calm down! What's wrong, what's happened?' He tried to get her to calm down but she was untameable, her whole body shaking uncontrollably. 'Mom! Mom what's going on?!' She finally became still and pulled away from Duncan, her breathing steadying. She looked deep into his eyes.

'They took her, Duncan...' she began weeping again as what she said became real to her, but she soon steadied again. 'My d-dealer, I told him I hadn't g-g-got the money to pay him, so h-he... Oh god Duncan they took Sophie!' She grasped him again but Duncan pushed her away.

'I told you this would happen Mom! Oh God, oh no, we have to do something... Have you called the police?' Duncan lowered his head, feeling utter shame. *It's my fault... I shouldn't have gone out this morning! How could I let this happen to poor Soph?*

'They said they w-w-would kill her if I called them, and if I don't get them the money in 24 h-h-hours.' The pain Duncan felt at this moment could not compare to any other; he couldn't stop thinking about her, how innocent she was, how confused she would be. What kind of a person would kidnap a 7 year old child?

Duncan looked at the ground and went over their options in his head, and with his new founded confidence he spoke 'Give me the address Mom. I'm going after them.'

He had no idea what was about to happen, his feelings were mixed and adrenalin surged through him; his No.1 priority was his sister. She didn't deserve any of this, and he would die before letting anything happen to her. He had to make it quick: get in, get Sophie, get out.

A block or two away he realised something; he had never before felt as confident and safe as he had when he was with Arturo. *Is asking him to come selfish? Should I be using him as my personal confidence booster?* He asked himself, but quickly pushed that thought to the back of his mind. The only way he was going to get through this was with the help of Arturo. His house wasn't much different than Duncan's, the state of the place showing the same lack of treatment. Arturo appeared at the door almost instantly, as if he had been waiting for Duncan to take him from this place.

Duncan rushed through the story at the door and Arturo was happy to come along, speaking of his own troubled times when having to confront his older brother's drug dealers. Winding down streets and dingy alleys they soon found themselves upon the doorstep of a long grey building, with music booming from the place. Duncan took a deep breath.

'Ready?'

'Ready as I'll ever be, amigo.' He nodded at Duncan. Duncan grasped the handle and pushed the door open with his body into a crowded hallway flooded with highly intoxicated people. He pushed his way through and started glancing into the rooms, trying to spot anyone who looked of a higher power. The intense music was pounding in his ears and the endless waves of people continued smashing into him, knocking him off balance several times. Eventually Arturo called his name over the blaring music, and he found his way to him.

They swung the door open with a quick tug, and drifted into the room. The scene was a mess, countless stains were sprayed across the wall and several African-American people were gathered beside one who Duncan assumed to be the leader. He was the only one sat down, and he looked as though he was a deranged king upon a throne of drugs and misery, and the men beside him the royal king's guard. Duncan quickly spotted his sister sat in the corner, her face red from tears. Duncan gathered all the confidence he had left and decided he needed to speak first, the leader's eyes staring upon him like an eagle's on its prey. 'I have come for my sister, and I'm not leaving here without her. My Mom is unable to pay you, but I promise we will pay you double if you wait.' Duncan was thinking that the money would merely be change once his career took off... If it took off.

The man stood up slowly, and Duncan motioned for Arturo to get Sophie. He did so without even a word from the leader or guards, just glances from emotionless eyes. After collecting her they both disappeared through the door and were swallowed into the crowd. The hint of a smirk flashed across the man's face and he began speaking in a deep, croaky voice 'Kid, I know you are trying to protect your family, and do you know what? I respect you for that. All this you see around you, all this I am doing for my family...' Duncan felt a pang of hope in his gut. 'However, I am afraid that business is business, and I need my money. Your mother has promised me many times that she would get me my money, and I gave her too many chances. She is not to be trusted, and I am not a charity! If she takes my things, I will take hers. However, it seems as though you have already decided to make my judgement for me. You took the girl and now you have to pay the price. I will get my compensation.' With that final word, he moved a hand down to the back of his jeans.

On impulse Duncan dived back into the crowd, and he heard several gunshots and screams come from behind him. The whole crowd surged towards the exit, blocking Duncan's path. He knew if he kept with the crowd it would end in his death, so he started looking frantically around the room for an escape. He spotted a smashed window several feet away from him, and vaulted through it without thought. Hopefully, they would think he was still in the crowd. He ran back onto the street and started sprinting away to the safety of his home. He had done it, he had gotten his sister out and they were both alive. Then he felt a sharp feeling smash him at the bottom of his spine. His whole body throbbed in pain, and he slammed to the ground, bringing the whole world crashing down with him…

He awoke to a bright light shining down at him, a cool breeze apparent upon his face. Was he dead? Was this Heaven, Hell? He tried to remember what had happened; *I got my sister out of the drug den, then I got myself out. But, why am I here if I got out safely? What happened?* Then the rest of the ceiling came into focus and he realised where he was. A hospital. It all came flooding back to him at once, he had been shot, the police arrived and he was rushed away in an ambulance. He wanted to see his sister, now. He attempted to move his legs, but nothing seemed to happen. He tried once more, then twice and many more after that. Then he tried moving the rest of his body and he got the same response, nothing. He finally admitted to himself the agonising truth; the bullet that hit him had paralysed him. His dream disappeared as quick as it had come, he would never play basketball again, never feel the thrill of a slam dunk. He was but a shell of his former self, a useless void of life.

After being thanked by his mother hundreds of times and being hugged by his sister the same amount, although he couldn't feel the hugs, he was finally met by an anxious Arturo. 'It's so good to see you man, if it wasn't for you my sister probably wouldn't be alive. I cannot thank you enough.' Duncan could feel tears welling in his eyes.

Arturo leaned in close to Duncan, tears suddenly streaming down his face

'Amigo, I am so sorry about what happened. Although we have
only known each other for a few days, you are the best friend I have ever had.' He looked directly into Duncan's eyes and a smirk formed on his lips

'And the greatest basketball player I have ever seen.' The sentence was so resolute it finally let the tears free, down Duncan's face. Duncan's gaze shifted away. 'I will never play it again though, nobody will even know me. I'm useless now... broken. They'll call me Duncan the Broken' Arturo's grin grew even wider, showing his surprisingly white teeth.

He knelt down to Duncan's level and began speaking.

'Duncan Smith, the skill and determination you showed when you beat Jackson was the single greatest display of basketball I have ever seen, and trust me, I have seen a lot.' He let out a small chuckle. 'I will make sure that nobody forgets the marvelousness you showed, I will make sure people know of your talent, I will get your story heard I promise you, muchacho. You will be as big as Michael Jordan, even bigger in fact! You are a hero, Duncan! You gave up your dream to save your loved ones... You will not be known as Duncan the Broken, you will be known, as Duncan the Proud!' And with that hey both laughed together. Duncan realised that everything *was* going to be okay.

See more titles
at
www.electragladepress.com

Caedmon College Creative Writing Group
Contact at
Caedmon College Whitby
Whitby
North Yorkshire
United Kingdom
www.ccwhitby.co.uk